The Shadow's Horse

The Shadow's Horse

Diane Glancy

The University of Arizona Press

Tucson

The University of Arizona Press
© 2003 Diane Glancy
First Printing
All rights reserved
∞ This book is printed on acid-free, archival-quality paper.
Manufactured in the United States of America

08 07 06 05 04 03 6 5 4 3 2 1

Library of Congress Cataloging-in-Publication Data
Glancy, Diane.
The shadow's horse / Diane Glancy.
p. cm.
ISBN 0-8165-2328-2 (pbk. : alk. paper)
I. Title.
PS3557.L294 S53 2003
811'.54—dc21
2002154914

British Library Cataloguing-in-Publication Data
A catalogue record for this book is available from the British Library.

Will thou break a leaf driven to and fro? —Job 13:15

Contents

Acknowledgments

Some of these poems have appeared previously in the following publications: *Alaska Quarterly Review* for "American Miniaturist"; *Caliban* for "Squaw" and "The Shadow's Horse"; *Confluence* for "Mammal Hall"; *Countermeasures* for "Words look for a place to belong"; *Dexter Review* for "Incursion"; *Field* for "The Great American Bottom"; *Furious Fictions* for *"A View of Colonel Johnson's Engagement with the Savages"; Furnitures: The Magazine of North American Ideophonics* for "Azalea Festival, Muskogee, Oklahoma"; *Indiana Review* for *"I raro te oviri"; Meadowlark* for "The Leaf Driver"; *Metis* for "Crackerjack" and "The Mounds Builders"; *Mother Superior* for "Because it was unto them"; *Paper Boat* for "Story"; *Pearl* for "Early Flight"; *POG* for "Curl" and "Tuning"; *Raven Chronicles* for "Story"; *Rhino* for *"Child with Doll";* and *The Heartlands Today* for "Driving."

Gratefulness to The Milton Center, Newman University, Wichita, Kansas, for second prize to *"Remuda"* in their poetry competition.

Acknowledgment to the Pablo Neruda Prize, *Nimrod International Journal of Poetry & Prose,* for "The Stockyard Series: Crow Standing Rez, They Handed Out Bible Verses like Oars, and *Remuda."*

Acknowledgment to the Poetry Society of America, for the Alice Fay Di Castagnola Award of finalist to an early version of the collection under the title, *American Miniaturist.*

The Shadow's Horse

Curl

A finch that learns the wrong song is in trouble. Apparently, every once in a while, instead of learning the song of his own father, a male finch learns the song of a neighbor; once in a blue moon, he learns the song of a neighbor of the wrong species.
—Jonathan Weiner, *The Beak of the Finch*

Once the leaves in a tree
then grounded to what
they don't know
curl their edges.

They belong to no one
of their particular kind.
*The shadow's horse
is a leaf,* they say,
raked into the decomposition of them
letting sun into the yard
running
broken.
If you line up all leaves that fall
how many times will they go around the earth?
What is a rake but a corral for leaves?
What is a horse?
A leaf?
The meaning of breaking?

Tuning

It was a life of exile under the trees.
My father came to the stockyards.
My mother from a farm.
In 1951 or 2 my parents flew from Kansas City to Indianapolis
to look for a house when my father was transferred.
I think of them far above me
small as birds when they flew,
and the earth to them was a sandbox in our backyard
where I made roads to a house I never found.
I often think of wives in tract houses.
The cows and pigs my father yarded
before they walked up the ramp to the kill.
Sometimes I thought we were together
because of something terrible we had done.
My father's Cherokee heritage tucked under
some sort of shame. The past _____
What was it? I call to them above me
no larger than a leaf.

Story

For Connie Hart, b. 1917, Lake Conda, who learned basket weaving by herself because her Koorie mother was not allowed to teach her in the mission. Connie's baskets now appear in the National Gallery of Victoria, Australia.

A woman makes a story because there's no shade, and you know how a story branches. A story's a tree unfolding. The leaves hide the sun beating. A story comes just like a tree where it stands after winter. The tree feels the sun through its bark. It feels the leaves pickaxing their way out. The tree moves all summer on those little plots called stems. You know some afternoons a story full of leaves and branching forks folds up and lifts. But there have to be leaves falling after the budding all summer. After the shade to stand between. Then rakes gather meaning. Not from a tree out of leaves, but from moving to story again. The woman says when it's cold, the bark looks like a column of hard, dark flames. In winter you can hold your hand to a tree.

American Miniaturist

She is
smaller than
history, her
acts of
childbirth not
recorded, her
acts of
obedience. How
severely she
is captured
by oil
paint on
a small
oval, hair
parted up
the middle,
tied behind
her head
to hold
her ears
open to
his voice,
which is
something like
a sidewalk
crusted after
sleet on

snow. Her
own voice
is a
pile of
leaves whose
tongues are
veined and
forked after
Indian wars,
stuffed into
the puppet
of her
mouth, a
sock-monkey twisted
and knotted
in a
shape not
its own.

Fit

To make her portrait fit the room, she made the house small, chairs small, the sofa. She made the children small as shoes she dried in the oven.

Our trips to the museum: the halls and empty rooms, the high ceilings, the furnitureless place: *imagine it small,* she said, so small she could hold the museum in her hand. Just look at the gathering of miniaturists: George Catlin, John Copley, Thomas Cummings, William Dunlap, Charles Fraser, George Freeman, Robert Fulton, Ann Hall, Henry Inman, John Jarvis, Edward Malbone, Anna Peale, James Peale, Henry Pelham, Gilbert Stuart, Thomas Sully, Benjamin Trott, John Trumbull, Benjamin West, Joseph Wood; their portraitures nailed there; there were others many others, their little brushes like leaves in a forest the trees too many to mention in this small space this small.

Remuda

I. Rapture

On the edge of town
my father in the stockyards
drove cattle up the ramp.
I could hear the feedlot and cattle pens.
I could hear the remuda.
The street near our house
climbed a hill
where a convent bell cut the neighborhood
with its butcher knife.
The sun stepped its hissing foot into puddles
like tanks steaming hair off hide.
Sometimes I put my fingers in and out my ears
to trill the *screech scrawl yawwk* of the locusts
as summer slipped into the closet like a moth.
Then old houses huddled like women
holding buffalo scrapers.
The first snow traveled over the plains
on clouds heavy as cattle cars.
Vaqueros rode the wind to the west;
their lariats, the leaves that fell.
I thought of Christ in the convent
sacrificed like cattle
when the sky unloaded its burden of sun
at vespers.
Then locust shells

hung empty on the bark
as if Christ stepped from his cross,
cracked the wafer sky
thin and transparent at dusk.

II. Processional

The cattle go up the ramp
dragging their crosses.
Their voices are Gregorian chants
rising to the blue sky,
the cold clouds.
Their eyes are wide and white.
The cows are on flame.
They will go wild into heaven
where places are set
in rippling tents
with tables and folding chairs
and placards with their names.
A fish will be tied on their heads.
They will hold corn in their mouths.
It is faith then
that comes
to elevate the dead.

III. Bronc
from a Harvey Caplin photograph

The horse is suspended mid-air,
back arched as if bent in prayer,
hind legs pulled forward,
front legs back
in a giant X.
The horse is ethereal,
mouth opened,
eyes terrified at some holy revelation.
The cowboys surround him,
each pulling their ropes
as though the horse were a marionette.
The whole process of *breaking* caught in the photo
ripping *will* from horse
until ropes untied,
the horse limps to the remuda.
In the background,
the fence rails of the corral,
the X of boards on the gate,
the buckboard in the distance,
the dumb butte.

IV. Crucifixion

My father ran the freight elevator
in the stockyards.
Through the Depression
he moved up through departments,
breaking strike lines,
loading trucks.
One night a car stopped in front of our house
before moving on.
I remember my father in the dark
at the front window.
But the car drove off
and another house was bombed.
The packing house was brutal.
A death on the cross.
But my father made it to plant superintendent
and sat on the front porch
after his hernia operations
resting from his holy work:
the cattle crowned with thorns,
the hogs crucified.

V. Resurrection

Only tumbleweed blow across the feedlots now.
My father died when the stockyards were razed.
I visit his grave.
So this is the elevation
of his spirit to heaven.
No cattle cars,
no prods,
no ramps,
no knives in the throat or bullets in the head.
Christ of the offal.
Christ of the steam tank.
Christ of manure.

VI. Afterlife

In the afterlife the cattle
lick my father's hand.
He in turn licks them.
Here there is further resurrection.
The lame walk.
The blind see.
It is in the afterlife that all are healed.
A remuda from which you choose your ride.
It is in the estuaries of heaven
the loggia trills with insect and beast.
Vivace! Con brio!
Even men are there
just below the Chief
who is Christ and God the Father
and somewhere the Holy Ghost
pulling tongues off the old meat carts
that were first to open the gate.

Mammal Hall

In the album I'm left half-
under the border
the front of my dress
stuck in my underpants
shoes white as goodness
my new brother in my father's arms
a mother's shadow wedged
between my feet
my basket with eggs mottled as the moon
somewhere over us
I had dropped to the edge
of the picture
another baby up there now
the thin membrane of his head
the pulse under it
his spirit knocking
trying to get out.

Driving

The problem is leaves and the raking
of memory is an act unfolding what falls there

The object toward which the rake moves
is not what is there
but a verb following the subject of leaves
which points to the leaves as its object

The large maple in the yard larger than the yard
covering the neighbor's also but the leaves fall in yours
waves and waves of them waving on the lawn
the bare yard open to the sun which the tree
takes most of

The problem is leaves they come every year to the tree
and fall in the yard all fall
they change from green to red or green to yellow
maybe some only brown as a layer cake in the oven

A leaf tastes like ice cream
if you eat a grape with it

Leaves smell like the nouns they are
unfolding the memory of autumn
the problem of leaves
is a direct object of disaffection

Once you gave your sister-in-law some leaves
for her birthday
your brother said as if he didn't have enough in the yard
but they were red and her birthday was autumn

As you pull the rake
you receive the bundles you could call the post office
to pick up

Raking causes other words to happen
lawnings for instance
which could be a noun or possibly a verb
such as leaves *lawning* over the yard

What if your place in heaven depends on the leaves you rake?

It's the unreliability of words
their meanings like leaves that fall
in patterns unpatterned by the wind that blows
all the neighbors' leaves into your yard

At night you hear the claws of leaves running
up the street
they cling to your door trying to get in

Wars have been started by leaves

In dreams sometimes you rake in the afterlife
leaves never stop falling
you dream yourself as a series of rakings

Once the neighbors tried all day to load a jeep
with more than it could hold
they arranged and rearranged
and nothing would change the space in the jeep
but the thought of life as a series
of packings
the vehicle smaller than the cargo it has to carry

Is it only in America leaves are raked?

You think of Germany
where part of your ancestors came from the western border
of a forest
bearing rakes as they crossed the ocean in ships
because there were more leaves in America

The problem is leaves
the waves piled with them
dumped continually on the shore

You drive your car through leaves running across the street
like scuttling crabs

You get your bearings
in the cars you drive through leaves in America
the boyfriend's two-toned Impala
the green station wagon
and the brown one you drove out of the marriage

A word is more than the sound it makes
the passages of air pushed from the mouth
falling like leaves on the ear

The problem is leaves you cannot get away from them
crowding the yard like squatters you must rake

If the snow falls on them they are there all winter
and kill the grass under them
have you lifted a slab of leaves that have been frozen
all winter
have you seen the yard beneath the slab?

The problem is leaves that fall and fall each fall
and would sleep in your bed if you would let them

You hear the ocean as you rake
but more than water is the raking
of the first car that was your own
you were married and the young mother of children
and a retired military couple next door
sold you the car they had driven from California
a military-green Ford rusted from the salt air by the ocean
of the military base where they were stationed
and your husband bought it for you so you could go
to the store

That car is in the leaves you rake
the green leaves turning brown

The importance of leaves leaves desire
bitter in the yard
the sound of the rake through them
the clatter of an old battle
leaves fleeing the rake in retreat

What if the way you rake your leaves is the way you treat nations?

Somehow you remember how you wanted to drive the leaf truck
that drove through old neighborhoods
and called the leaves to it like the ice cream man
and the leaves would run
watch out you said as you watched them crushed
up into the leaf heaven you know is there

The Iliad is actually about leaves
the long war between the Greeks and Troy
Don Quixote was a leaf
the matadors from Spain
running leaves in the streets clicking their castanets.

Spain

This is the country they came from
civil war
inquisition
corruption
storks on the tower
of Capilla Universitaria de
San Ildefonso
in the great woven ships of their nests
where they stand as masts
above the calle Pedro Gumiel
students pass
on narrow streets
not looking at what surrounds them
bringing their new, blind world.

Overhead

The planes fly high as planes have to get
over the houses. There's something *thoral* in
their throats.
They rattle plates like the sun
standing in its groove on its shelf.
Our history begins in a word
spoken. Without dialogue
we perish though it seems we go anywhere
small as we are.
Now you remember
as the plane slides through different levels of space.
Nothing is anything in itself
but exists in a dialogue planning to return,
washed by the sky,
wiped by the moon.

Granted

Short notice yet
you knew it coming
ground (bare)
leaf (raked)
tree (branched)
if cherished
the distilled
yet not among
(outdoor) nations
the cleanup
a compost
a lap of raking
let me sit on
(all) of yesterday
shade
you can put
your hand (through).

Crow Standing Rez

We played stockyards
with our cardboard boxes
making cattle pens in the backyard.
Drovers came with herds,
then cattle cars on rails.
These river bottoms
at the confluence of the Missouri and Kaw,
the flood we washed over the stockyards
with the backyard hose.
The puddles we let dry.
Then carts of tails and intestines,
carts of tongues
making grooves on the wood floor of the packing house,
the raven-black knot of the heart.

They Handed Out Bible Verses like Oars

These are the beasts you shall eat: the ox, the sheep and the goat.
The hart, and the roebuck, and the fallow deer, and the wild goat, and
the pygarg. And every beast that parts the hoof, and chews the cud, you
shall eat.
—Deuteronomy 14:4–6

I. *The pygarg was a bison, or an antelope,* they said,
whatever they could think of at the given moment.

We walked the animals up the ramp
where God with a crimson underlining in his robe
opened a nostril and shot lightning out.
The clouds were white as butcher paper.
The rain fell as darkened knives.

Christ in the tomb wore butcher paper as interment cloth
when he traveled to the underworld to gather
the slaughtered animals who walked to the men with knives.

II. This shipwrecked
sail of butcher paper glazed with sleet
on the ocean does snow fall there?

For dinner on the tossing ship
here's what for—
a woman in a blue dress
slicing the ship's log on a table

beating it with the meat cleaver
the ax
and sharpened knife

the pages not a napkin on her lap.

III. *Migration of the Negro,* #1, Jacob Lawrence,
The Phillips Collection, Washington, D.C.

The woman is slicing a slab of bacon
but it looks like a book.
A boy stands by the table
his tongue against the tablecloth.

IV. My father is standing over the table cutting a slab of bacon,
his head bowed so low it looks like there is nothing on his
shoulders
but my father is cutting a book.
Outside there is snow covering the yard and trees like butcher
paper.
I hear the shovel on the walk *thusch thusch* into the snow,
lifting, tossing it to the side,
the snow jumping from the shovel
as if children in their trunks at a wading pool
the swirl of blue cold against the window.

The house had curtains of butcher paper
the tables were troughs for blood
from throats when hoisted with chains upside down
like apostles
fiery angels cut loose.

I raro te oviri (Under the Pandanus)

Paul Gauguin, 1848–1903
Dallas Museum of Art

Think of the snowy landscape. The delicate spots falling, cornering the ground. The bleached weeds, the white side of a shed. The dark stakes in the garden like crosses. Snow on chicken wire. One touch and it would fall. How the fragments join together on the ground. How it all comes back in different form. Those two under the screw pines. Food gathering. *I raro te oviri.* The awkward blackness of their night. The cloisonné branches. Tropical pandanus bowing to the fact. The dog like a spill of Pennzoil. The stains of red. Chartreuse. Yellows. Under them. First man and woman. She with the guilt of her fault. Then the redemption. The invisible whiteness of faith. The net of the matter covering. Just imagine the sorrows lifted. Burdens scattered. The white. Pure white hope.

A View of Colonel Johnson's Engagement with the Savages (Commanded by Tecumseh) near the Moravian Town, October 5, 1812

Henry Trumbull, 1781–1843
St. Louis Art Museum

The painting is numbered so you see what's happening.

1. Colonel Johnson heroically defending himself against the attack of an Indian chief

2. The American Infantry firing upon a body of the enemy on the left

3. A dismounted Dragoon personally engaged with one of the enemy

4. The cavalry pursuing the retreating savages across the hills

5. Tecumseh rallying his men, and encouraging them to return to the attack

6. A savage in the act of scalping a wounded drummer of the American Infantry

7. The savages, pursued by the cavalry, retreating to a swamp on the left

8. The enemy (rallied by their commander Tecumseh) returning to the attack

Otherwise you might not get through the scenes of action.

The central horses with their men
the outer trees
the woods and far cornfields
Indians dying under puffs of musket smoke.

You know you remember by numbers. You see there are whole stories not told here.
It's what you mean when you say whole geese picked up a swamp and Hagonwhatha crossed dry ground. Those are the stories like that.

1. Hagonwhatha wanted to go and didn't want to get wet
2. Or build a raft
3. Or not cross at all

The flock of geese flying with the swamp like a blanket under their feet. Hagonwhatha crossing, picking up swamp grass to take to the other side. Thinking how often the deck was stacked.

The leaves crushed under the rake of their moving

History (American)
shoots a pellet _____
to the head
covers war trails
massacres
land allotments
now re-pile
the piled leaves
the leaf piles (of them).
Restand the fallen
look at the ground
beneath
they are savage
that dance
to their tune.

Leafers

Over the years the leaves on the lawn
raked into I can't help but think
we gave our lives
to the red coats of them
coming
so many groupings
into which raked raked raked raked raked raked raked
raked raked raked raked raked raked raked raked raked raked
raked raked raked raked raked
everything of value
we finally learn
the corridors of trees
the small (self) portrait
of the leaves.

Because it was unto them

she had to walk on marbles that were hurtful as well as slippery. Because her house was a floor of marbles hard as waves, because the marbles had glass swirls in them she saw them as a thousand earths. And because they were under her feet, the clouds came and lived in her head. The Thunder Beings and Lightning. The Lightning first because it was faster. Snake-tongued and zipping out. The slower Thunder Beings because they were burdened with the Lightning's sound. *Thunder. Thunder,* the Thunder Beings said. They rumbled from her mouth. It was the high atmosphere. The clouds swarming bees inside her head. The Lightning shooting from her eyes. It cracked the marbles until the swirls high-tailed it over the heavens in her head. Far above the sharp waves of glass on the floor so broken she couldn't separate one from the other. All grinding her feet as she walked the broken earths. Spilling her blood. While Thunder Beings stormed from her mouth.

Crackerjack

The woman's lost her grip. She's
7-Up and whatever it takes to mean.
Lord ho. A dislocated shoulder.
A Fig Newton. And why does
she have to be *sok ejaborated?*
Also out of tune. You'd think
she'd have it straight by now.
Her own language. Her own space.
Bless her. The woman's lived like a
hived bee. A hoed fence.
Whose life is a wash day before
rural electrification. Whose *songues*
rise against the dawn. Bless her *some-
day freed-way. Her hoopla. High-
roll.* It's still ahead.
Her *jam-snort. Hip-bang. Blow-out.
Hoe-down. Wingding. Pow Wow.*
All her *fiestivity.*

Azalea Festival, Muskogee, Oklahoma

In the haymounds of our history,
shelves in the house of fruit jars,
jellies of summers in the kitchen.
After we moved from life the lone
elm jammed the screen. The
cordial sky patrolled our past.
Now the rush pleasure goes by with.
Space adheres to the flowers
a moment. Then the remnant
slivered-off for walls
between our rooms.

The Great American Bottom

(The alluvial plain in southern Illinois between the bank of the
Mississippi and the bluffs that border the prairie to the east)

The old cafe received the detritus
between the counter and front window.
Just in time she realized the strength
of her alluvium.
To be the great land the river flowed by,
to know the joy of goodness
that soaks within.
She held her wind and whistled to herself.
Her lungs soft bread boxes.
Her kneecaps bags of yeast.
It was the inner landscape of the mind
scraped clean of crumbs,
the edges of piecrust crimped.
The lovely, yes, the lovely booth.
Who couldn't hope to wish
or to hop back for anything but *obquesence?*
All the burning on the rack.
Yet she knew the showers in the girls' gyms,
the chlorine-smelling ovens.
Crookneck squash. Hoecakes. Meat pies.
She could *enumberate* them.
She's the woman swimming in the inner ear.
The figure mother in apron, hairnet,
taking orders from the river,
the rascal passing river.

The Mounds Builders

(It was along the Great American Bottom that the Mounds Builders
reached their highest civilization.)

In the bathroom she scrubbed us
under the fingernails,
behind the ears,
anything to wash off the difference.
She picked up our words and put them back
into our mouths,
said *come in here* from the kitchen
as she fed us eggs and toast,
working all the time around the mouth,
the throat,
handing us the napkin
for the eraser bits like crumbs.

Incursion

You see a girl in a photo
and think of her under dark and fog
and the limbs of pines pushing down.
Not the constellation of a cotton field
that could touch your heart,
that could knock your head in two.

But now you feel there is order
growing over the hillside holding down
the soil under trees.
You have a small place in the tight pines,
a narrow road, the full air,
the first turn of autumn sweeping southward.
You wake with a constant heart,
claim deaf rocks, the land
too dear to hold.
You could almost forget
the fields of cotton floating under
the eye, the girl you never were again.

Mummified

Nancy Spero, 1926–
Museum of Contemporary Art, Chicago

The museum of her words stays with you.
The playground where a flag cut the air.
A mother's battlefield we carried to school.
Her vacuum cleaner encased in the closet.
She bobbed like the bulb in the tank.
Her war series was something
you didn't walk away from.
Paintings on the wall like windows of a plane
when you're going somewhere,
usually back
over the roof
where nightly you lifted a white flag.

                During recess
                we had a game.
The girls stood in line along the fence. The boys made a wall
against the other. The boys crossed one at a time and pulled us
to their side. Our job was to resist, to struggle and buck against
them, which we did. And if we got loose, we ran back to our
side. But 1 x 1 they dragged us across the playground with
skinned knees, scuffed shoes, until the teachers, embalmed and
wrapped with gauze as they were, wouldn't let us play this new
game, this beast we unfurled.

Early Flight

The spotted scenery,
the clouds full of white foliage.
Something mother would have pointed out
years ago on a trip through the mountains.
And I in the backseat
reading a magazine thinking about the boy
I'd left the night before,
would look up at the strip of sky,
the hilltop of trees,
the back of my father's head.
And folding the other leg under me
I would feel the ache my boyfriend left for days.

Now the plane up over the clouds
on a new morning.
The raw sky as if something primitive and wild,
a canyon drawn by someone who didn't know
what he was doing,
or an abstract with a notch of trees
or a wolf howl.
Then the sudden opening of a wet road,
engineers still looking into the surveyor's level
trying to find a way through the next layer
of hills
the trees
the land below like my boyfriend's
camouflage jacket

as he hunched over the target range
at National Guard camp,
a strange marksman like the wind
rippling the pages of my magazine,
the neck of my blouse.

Gertrude

Red Grooms, 1937–
The University of Iowa Museum of Art, Iowa City

Don't waste the leaves, she said,
and raked and raked.
The afternoons they fled from trees
she chased after them into traffic.
In the yard she raked them back under the tree.
She tried to hang the wind from the fence
by the tail with the opossum.
She called to each leaf, *dear one.*
We could hear her voice
crying for the leaves
crumbled under the car tires and crushed
by the weight of her heart.
Day and night we heard the yard rake scratching,
going at it, getting out the knots,
the tender feelings under the scalp,
each vein and leafstalk, the root and head lice.

The Goodnight Trail

We became the cows we killed
our tongues thick and black
jaws squared
we ate one another
as they ate in church
their god
tail and hoof
nightmares
the knife/saw/ax
here moocow, they said
swallow this one more
spoonful after this
take any massacre
the rain our only water trough
a quick dose of cough syrup
then the coughing stopped.

The Lamentations of Cattle

Her gates are sunk into the ground;
he has destroyed and broken her bars.
—Lamentations 2:9

We unloaded them from cattle trucks.
Their legs gave way.
They stumbled and were prodded to stand.
Their groans were the stars rubbed together.
Their smell was in our nose.
Surely pain and suffering went with them;
they dwelled with fear in their sight.

From above he sent fire into their bones (Lamentations 1:13).
Their towers fell.
They were the cattle of his pasture,
now they were desolate.

The Lord is their portion;
therefore they hope in him (Lamentations 3:24).

A Box of Negatives

They knew _____ was coming.
Then darkroom blackness.
Their legs quivered a brief ghost dance
they didn't have a _____.
Others pushing from behind
like children shuffling in a cafeteria line.
It was quick as _____
what (was) it?
Whippoorwill? Was it
clouds white as bone fertilizer
thunder of rail cars
bringing the little cows to their beds?

Small Horse

He may not be the smallest horse
but in the trailer there is hay and he steps into it
never remembering what gets him
where he doesn't want to go
then the gate is up
the truck is start
and he is at rodeo
ridden
if only he could remember
not to follow the hay
into a box with wheels hooked to truck.
Could he go over these lessons enough?
The ride across dust
boxed in the hot
only wanting his water trough
the breath of wind set loose in a shingle of his shed
only he hears.

Portraiture

Just right now I can't
say what I mean
no more than
tell me around the corner
there is not a leaf
you page them in your books
study them as maps.

Tulsa Burning, 1921

from an interview with Eldoris McCrondichie, abcnews.com

Telephone poles
houses
burning
all I could see was black smoke
rolling
one house blown up
but the fragment
of a curtain
where they kept the fireplace and two
small windows
on each side
just a piece of curtain blowing
a smoke signal
or a leaf.

Child with Doll

Milton Avery, 1893–1965
Philbrook Museum of Art, Tulsa

The doll looks more like the child
the child blockish

and more like the doll.
In the corner

the sun is wax-papering
the sky.

Something like branches streak
the child's mouth

purple as a jelly sandwich.
The child's arms could be

ramps or long chutes.
The doll could be

thinking she would fall
if the child leaned forward reaching.

Leafing

I rake the yard
wearing my wool
blue gloves.
The leaves pile like an ocean.
I uncover the
bare spots with my boat.
King of bees.
How can anyone be holy?
I rake the waves
I heard in the trees
all night.
I drive them to the leaf dump.
They buzz over
a railroad track,
the bumps in the road.
They rustle like candy
in their plastic
sacks I carry
with my blue gloves
from the deepest part
of the ocean.

Words look for a place to belong

That's what story is. Words trying to hold other words. On a trip to New Zealand when all you have to say is, *this is beautiful, the Southern Alps go on and on, snow capped and mountain streamed,* you look for something more. You know the sheep you saw from the small plane in Teanau looked like rice scattered in a field. You tell your words to keep working. You say their voice is a waterfall on granite, which over time makes a Brancusi sculpture of a gorge in southern New Zealand. It's nothing they don't know themselves. Words seek transformation. They seek connectives. Sometimes you find them *transpotted.* You stand on a gravel plain the glacier left between the mountains. You feel the altitude of cold. Later from a plane you see over and over the streambeds curve in the gravel like the curls in Maori art. But how was it seen from the height? Maybe words climb. Maybe they come back and say what it was like. They put their fingers on Milford Sound, NZ. Or your memory of it. You feel the sea level rise on the mountains. You see their peaks hooked like tongues sputtering for air. Old tongues speaking above the water, struggling since the beginning to speak.

Hyde Park Barracks, Macquarie Street, Sydney

It was a hard place
with hammocks strung like boat hulls.

There were orphans from the workhouse
and unprotected women.

Sarah Wood was one who came 1861,
died 1868,

sewed with the song of lice in her head.
Rats' feet ran the floor

while she dreamed
of bride's lace covering her ears.

A flowering bush maybe just imagined
in the spring yard.

There were baths once a week,
hot or cold, whatever the mistress decided.

At night she heard the rats stealing her scraps
and material bits for their wedding nests.

Across the street,
the ringing of St. Mary's Church.

Foliage

The surface of the ocean is fractured
with a thousand pieces of water

as if leaves on a tree
as if leaves on many trees

as if the ocean were a moving forest
the great waves

its branches
so many trees they are no longer trees

but Primal Tree
in a dream from the dark

and wet unknowing
where birds swim limb to limb

the way the form of things
is rearranged in dreams

turned sideways doesn't connect
taking over the bare space.

Nothing grows on the water
they have tried for years

but after the boats plow
the water remains barren

except in idea
or the image of idea

the great trunk growing up
from the bottom

or maybe down from the sky
the great invisible trunk

the everything
the everywhere.

The Shadow's Horse

In my heart there's a horse riding over the hill. Over its heart there's a minute silver speck of a plane. It has just come from nursing at the gate of a city. *Whoa!* says the horse to itself, for it has no rider. But it thinks it does, you see, for wholeness in a horse's heart is when its shadow and its rider's are one. It is another stock of horse since the new age has set in. Its ears are tepees on a hill. Maybe now the horse is a sculptor, and what it makes it becomes. But one leg won't stay on, or maybe it is hollow. Nevertheless, it drives its hooves into the ground and over the hill that is my heart, its leap cajoles the sun.

The Leaf Driver

I've been out raking leaves by now it's noon and more are on the tree. I drive the bags I have raked to the compost and return. It doesn't stop them from coming soon the yard is full again.

I ask what lesson there is in this. A silver maple spreading its droppings over my yard; this animal leaving its tracks. A tree spreads its shade in summer, which is raked up in the fall. I could say the air is falling in my yard with a tangibleness from God that has to be raked.

The rake is an oar going upriver. Through the unanswerable trees, the indiscernible exactness of a warm day late in autumn, which is usually cold.

The sound of the rake in the small yard enclosed by a wooden fence. The shade of the fence, the shadows of branches on the fence. The leaves falling one by one, slipping their shade through the air.

Squaw

A squawl a squawk or inbetween. I'll do it then. Pick up the earth, roll it under a bush beside the cornfield marked with furrows. I can say how to take the language, blow it like a brown paper sack, hit it with my hands. I am the remainder after my numbers won't come out right. Not a voice of absolute or aggression, but this is my bowl, *haka,* this is my bowl.

About the Author

Diane Glancy is a Professor at Macalester College in St. Paul, Minnesota, where she teaches Native American Literature and Creative Writing. Her latest novels are *The Man Who Heard the Land, Designs of the Night Sky, The Mask Maker,* and *Stone Heart: A Journal of Sacajawea.* She has also published a collection of six plays titled *American Gypsy,* and two recent collections of poetry, *The Relief of America* and *Stones for a Pillow,* which won the Stevens Poetry Award from the National Federation of State Poetry Societies. Glancy has received an American Book Award, a National Endowment for the Arts Fellowship, a Minnesota State Arts Board Grant, and a McKnight Fellowship/Loft Award of Distinction in Creative Prose. She is of Cherokee and German/English heritage. She received a 2001 Cherokee Medal of Honor from the Cherokee Honor Society in Tahlequah, Oklahoma, and a 2001 Thomas Jefferson Teaching Award from Macalester College. Glancy received her M.F.A. from the University of Iowa.